CW01507800

CONTENTS

MASTERING MECHANICS 1

OCR SYLLABUS

YOUR FAST TRACK

TO A-LEVEL SUCCESS

THE MATHS CLINIC

ISBN-10:1530372143
ISBN-13:978-1530372140

DEDICATED TO THE SERIOUS STUDENT

"It takes a lot of hard work to make something simple"

-Steve Jobs-

THE M.T.V. METHOD
Memorise . Test . Validate

Drawing from years of teaching Mathematics, The Maths Clinic has devised a foolproof method to master mathematical concepts for success in exams.

Armed with pen and notepad, follow this three-step M.T.V. method for each chapter:

A set of key points encapsulates each mathematical topic. Take time to commit this key list to memory. The success of your exam preparation depends on this step. Master the basics and you will master Mathematics.

The test page checks your assimilation of the key points for the chapter. Associated with each key point is a key question. Work through the test questions diligently.

TEST

Check the answers to all the key questions here. The answer page includes step by step working of each question.

VALIDATE

We recommend a thorough exam preparation to include the following:
Step 1: Master the key points using the M.T.V. Method.
Step 2: Answer at least five past exam question papers completely and within the prescribed time

1. KINEMATICS OF A PARTICLE

1.1 KEY POINTS

1. Symbols used and what they represent:

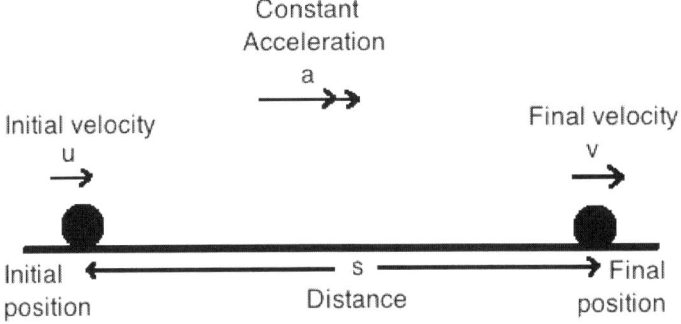

s – displacement or distance (metres)

u – initial velocity (metres per second ms^{-1})

v – final velocity (metres per second ms^{-1})

a – constant acceleration (metres per second^2 ms^{-2})

t – time (seconds)

Convert all measurements into the SI units of metres and seconds.

2. For a particle moving horizontally in a straight line with constant acceleration, we have the following:

   a. Displacement and velocity are positive when the particle moves from left to right and negative when the particle moves from right to left.

   b. If a particle is slowing down it has negative acceleration or deceleration.

c. For solving problems about particles moving in a straight line with constant acceleration, use the following formulae:

$$v = u + at$$

$$s = \frac{(u+v)t}{2}$$

$$v^2 = u^2 + 2as$$

$$s = ut + \frac{1}{2}at^2$$

$$s = vt - \frac{1}{2}at^2$$

3. For a particle moving vertically in a straight line with constant acceleration, we have the following:

a. There is a constant downward acceleration due to gravity $g = 9.8\ ms^{-2}$.

b. When solving problems about vertical motion, the positive direction can be chosen to be either upwards or downwards.

c. For objects projected upwards, $g = -9.8\ ms^{-2}$. For falling objects, $g = 9.8\ ms^{-2}$.

d. Projections

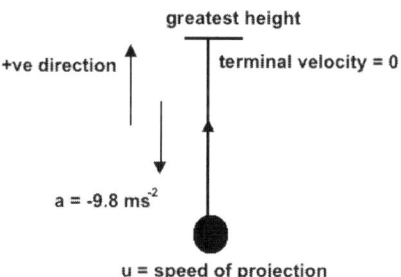

i.   The total time that an object is in motion from the time it is projected upwards to the time it hits the ground is called the time of flight.

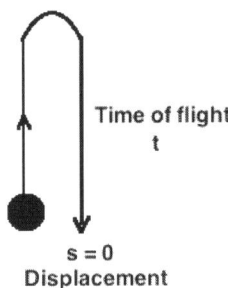

ii. The initial speed is called the speed of projection.

iii. The displacement of an object that is projected and returns to its original position is taken as zero $(s = 0)$.

iv. If the original projected position is $X\ m$ above the returning position, the displacement is taken as $-X$ $(s = -X)$.

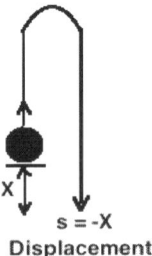

4. Speed-Time graphs

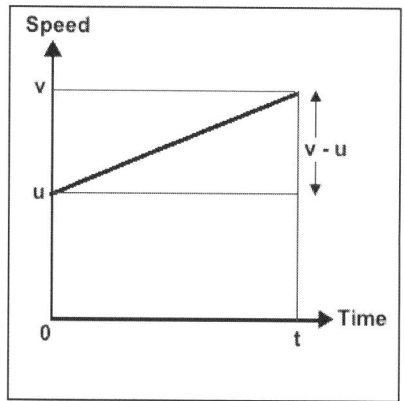

a. The motion of an object can be represented by a speed - time graph. Time is always plotted on the $x-axis$, Speed is plotted on the $y-axis$.

b. The gradient of a speed - time graph is the acceleration

$$a = \frac{(v-u)}{t}$$

c. A straight line indicates a constant or uniform acceleration.

d. The area under a speed – time graph is the distance travelled. Negative areas imply negative distance.

$$s = \frac{(u+v)t}{2}$$

(s is the area of the trapezium with height t and parallel

sides u and v)

e. Integrating a function of velocity also gives the distance travelled.

$$s = \int_0^t v(t)dt$$

5. Distance – Time graphs

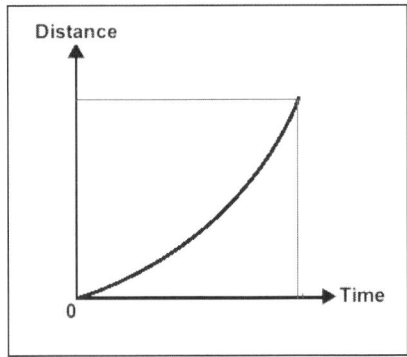

a. The motion of an object can be represented by a distance - time graph. Time is always plotted on the x–axis, Distance is plotted on the y–axis.

b. The gradient of a distance - time graph is the velocity. $Speed = \frac{Distance}{Time}$

c. A straight line indicates a constant speed, a curve indicates an acceleration or a deceleration.

6. Acceleration – Time graphs

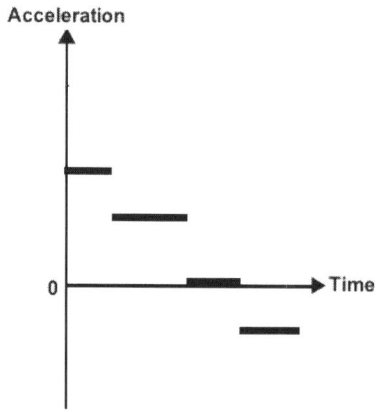

a. The motion of an object can be represented by an acceleration - time graph. Time is always plotted on the x–axis, Acceleration is plotted on the y–axis.

b. The gradient of an acceleration - time graph is 0.

c. The area under an acceleration – time graph is the change of velocity.

7. Given the distance s and time t, we have the following:

Velocity $v = \frac{ds}{dt}$ therefore $\int v\, dt = s$

Acceleration $a = \frac{dv}{dt} = \frac{d^2s}{dt^2}$ therefore $\int a\, dt = v$

1.2 TEST YOURSELF

1. Define the symbols s, u, v, a and t and state the SI units for each.

2. For a particle moving horizontally in a straight line with constant acceleration, which movement makes the displacement and velocity positive and which movement makes the displacement and velocity negative?

3. If a particle is slowing down describe its acceleration.

4. State the 5 formulae used in solving problems about particles moving in a straight line with constant acceleration.

5. What is the acceleration due to gravity?

6. Define time of flight in a projection.

7. Define speed of projection.

8. What is the displacement of an object that is projected and returns to its original position?

9. What is the displacement of an object that is projected if the original projected position is X m above the returning position?

10. Sketch a speed-time graph.

11. What is the gradient of a speed-time graph?

12. What does the area under a speed-time graph define?

13. What does integrating a function of velocity result in?

14. Sketch a distance-time graph.

15. What is the gradient of a distance-time graph?

16. Sketch an acceleration-time graph.

17. What is the gradient of an acceleration-time graph?

18. Given the distance s and time t, state the relation between the acceleration, the velocity and the distance.

19. A particle is moving in a straight line with constant acceleration. The points P, Q and R lie on this line. The particle moves from P through Q to R. The speed of the particle at P is 3 ms^{-1}and the speed of the particle at Q is 8 ms^{-1}. The particle takes 15s to move from P to Q.

    a. Find the acceleration of the particle.

    b. The speed of the particle at R is 12 ms^{-1}. Find the time taken for the particle to move from Q to R.

    c. Find the distance between P and R.

20. A ball is projected vertically upwards from a point O and rises to a maximum height of 10 m above O. The ball is modelled as a particle moving freely under gravity.

    a. Show that the speed of projection is 14 m s^{-1}.

    b. Find the time, in seconds, when the ball is 8.4 m above O.

21. A particle moves along a straight line and accelerates uniformly from rest to a speed of 6 ms^{-1} in T seconds. It then travels at a constant speed of 6 ms^{-1} for 3T seconds and decelerates uniformly to rest in 20 s. The total distance travelled by the particle is 480 m.

    a. Sketch a speed–time graph to illustrate the motion of the particle.

    b. Find the value of T.

c. Sketch an acceleration–time graph to illustrate the motion of the particle.

22. The velocity v m s^{-1} of a particle moving in a straight horizontal line at time t seconds is given by v = 4t^2 – 6t + 2. Initially, the particle has a displacement of 5 m from a fixed point O on the line.

a. Find the initial velocity of the particle.

b. Show that the particle is at rest when t = 1 and find the other value of t when it is at rest.

c. Find the displacement of the particle from the fixed point O when t = 6.

1.3 ANSWERS

Questions 1-18: Check Key Points for answers.

19.

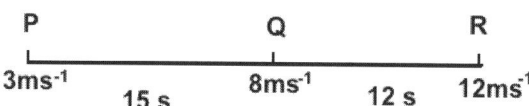

a.

$u = 3\ m\ s^{-1}$

$v = 8\ m\ s^{-1}$

$t = 15\ s$

$v = u + at$

Acceleration of the particle a is given by

$$a\ =\ \frac{v-u}{t}\ =\ \frac{8-3}{15}\ =\ \frac{1}{3}m\ s^{-2}\ =\ 0.33\ m\ s^{-2}$$

b. $u = 8\ m\ s^{-1}$

$v = 12\ m\ s^{-1}$

$a = 0.33\ m\ s^{-2}$

$v = u + at$

Time taken to move from P to Q is given by t

$$t\ =\ \frac{v-u}{a}\ =\ \frac{12-8}{0.33}\ =\ 12\ s$$

c. $s = ut + \frac{1}{2}at^2$

$t = 15 + 12 = 27\ s$

$u = 3\ m\ s^{-1}$

$a = 0.33 ms^{-2}$

Distance between P and R is given by s

$$s = (3 \times 27) + \frac{1}{2} \times \frac{1}{3} \times 27^2$$

$s = 81 + 121.5 = 202.5$ m

20.

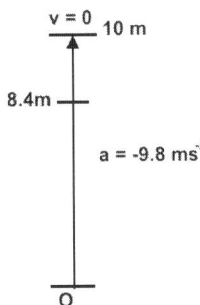

a. $v^2 = u^2 + 2as$

     $u^2 = v^2 - 2as$

     $= 0 - [2 \times (-9.8) \times 10]$

     $= 196$

     Speed of projection is given by u

     $u = \sqrt{196} = 14$ m s^{-1}

b. $s = 8.4$ m

     $u = 14 \, ms^{-1}$

     $a = -9.8 \, ms^{-2}$

     $s = ut + \frac{1}{2}at^2$

$8.4 = 14t + \frac{1}{2}(-9.8)t^2$

$4.9\ t^2 - 14t + 8.4 = 0$

Multiplying by 10 and dividing by 7 we have:

$7t^2 - 20t + 12 = 0$

Factorising we have:

$(7t - 6)(t - 2) = 0$

Time when the ball is 8.4m above O is t

$t = 2\ s, t = 0.86\ s$

21.

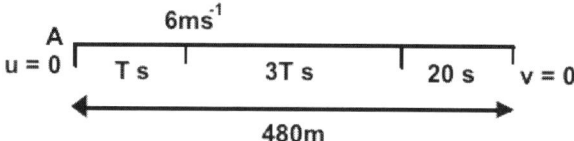

a.

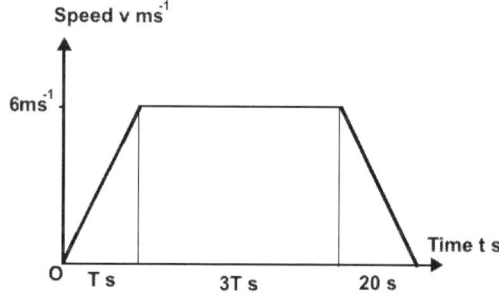

b. Distance travelled by particle = Area of trapezium (Area under graph)

Area of trapezium $= \frac{1}{2}h(a + b)$ where h is the height and a and b are the two parallel sides

Height of trapezium $= 6$

Lengths of the two parallel sides are $(T + 3T + 20)$ and $3T$

$D = \frac{1}{2}6(T + 3T + 20 + 3T)$

$D = 3(7T + 20) = 480$

$21T + 60 = 480$

$21T = 420$

$T = 20$ s

c. Acceleration-time graph

Given $T = 20$s, the duration of the three phases now works out to $T = 20$s, $3T = 60$s and 20s.

Using the formula $a = (v - u)/t$ we calculate the acceleration for each time period.

Period 1 (Time: 20 s): $u = 0$, $v = 6$, $t = 20$

hence $a = 6/20$ m s^{-2} $= 0.33$ m s^{-2}

Period 2 (Time: 60 s): $u = 6$, $v = 6$, $t = 60$

hence $a = 0$ m s^{-2}

Period 3 (Time: 20 s): $u = 6$, $v = 0$, $t = 20$

hence $a = -\frac{6}{20}$ m s^{-2} $= -0.33$ m s^{-2}

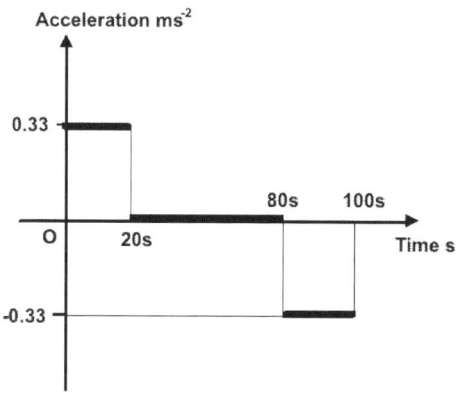

22.

a. Velocity v = 4t² – 6t + 2

   Initial Velocity u is obtained for t = 0

   u = 2 ms⁻¹

b. At rest 4t² – 6t + 2 = 0

   Factorising we have (2t – 2)(2t – 1) = 0

   Besides t = 1 we also have t = $\frac{1}{2}$

c. Distance $s = \int v\, dt$

$$s = \int (4t^2 - 6t + 2)dt$$

$$s = \frac{4t^3}{3} - \frac{6t^2}{2} + 2t + c$$

When t = 0, s = 5 giving us c = 5 in the above equation.

$$\therefore s = \frac{4t^3}{3} - \frac{6t^2}{2} + 2t + 5$$

Substituting in the above equation for t = 6, we have:

s = 288 – 108 + 12 + 5 = 197m

2. NEWTON'S LAWS OF MOTION

2.1 KEY POINTS

1.   Newton's first law: Objects in motion tend to stay in motion and objects at rest tend to stay in rest unless acted upon by an unbalanced force.

2.   Newton's second law: Force equals mass times acceleration.

3.   Newton's third law: For every action there is an equal and opposite reaction.

4.   The unit of force is the Newton N. It is defined as the force that will cause a mass of 1kg to accelerate at the rate of 1 m s^{-2}.

5. $F = ma$ is the equation of motion. F is the force in Newtons, m is the mass of the object in kg and a is the acceleration in m s^{-2}.

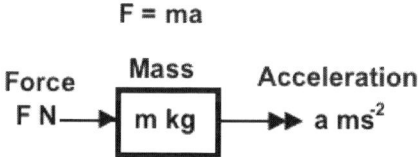

6. The weight of an object W is the force due to gravity acting on it. W = *mg*. W is the force in Newtons, *m* is the mass of the object in kg and *g* is the acceleration due to gravity = 9.8 m s^{-2}.

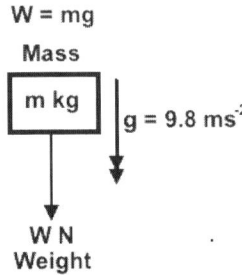

7. The normal reaction R is the force equal in magnitude to the weight W of the object.

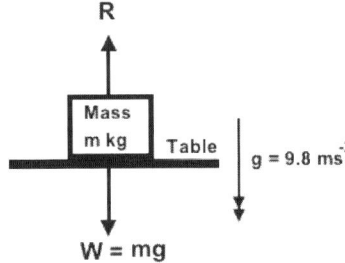

8.   When more than one force acts on an object, the resultant force is usually resolved in the direction of the acceleration and perpendicular to the acceleration. The resultant force is symbolically represented by R and an arrow indicating the direction of resolution: $R(\uparrow), R(\downarrow), R(\rightarrow), R(\leftarrow)$.

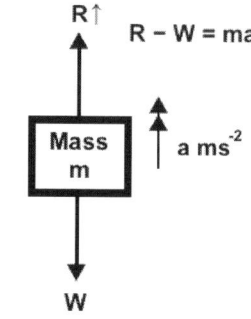

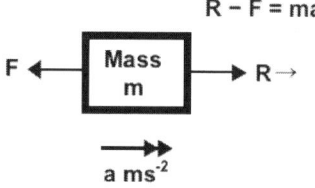

2.2 TEST YOURSELF

1. State Newton's three laws of motion.

2. Define a Newton.

3. State the relation between the force F, the mass m and the acceleration a.

4. Give the formula for the weight W of a body of mass m.

5. Define the normal reaction R.

6. When more than one force acts on an object, how is the resultant force usually resolved?

7. Standard problems involving the equations of motion:

a.   Lift problems:

A person weighing 80kg travels in a lift. What is the force exerted by the floor of the lift on the person in the following instances?

   i.   The lift moves upwards with an acceleration of 4 ms^{-2}.

   ii. The lift moves downwards with an acceleration of
        $5\ ms^{-2}$.

b.   Connected object problems:

A car of mass 1000 kg is towing a trailer of mass 600 kg along a straight horizontal road. The trailer is connected to the car by a tow rope which is parallel to the direction of motion of the car and the trailer. The engine of the car provides a constant driving force of 5000 N. The trailer exerts a resistance of 600N to the motion of the car. What is the acceleration of the car and the tension in the tow rope?

c. Problems with a pulley and two objects

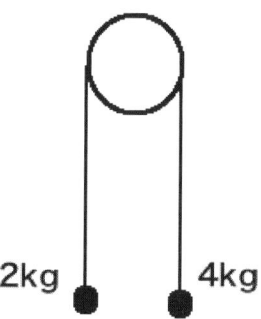

Particles of mass 2 kg and 4 kg are connected by a light inextensible string passing over a smooth, light pulley. The particles are released from rest with the string taut and the hanging parts of the string vertical, as shown in the figure. Calculate the tension in the string and the acceleration of the system.

d. Pulley and table problem

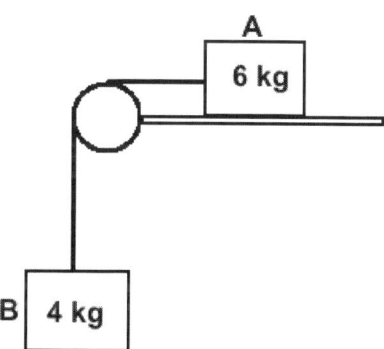

Two particles A and B of masses 6 kg and 4 kg respectively are attached to the ends of a light inextensible string. Particle A is held at rest on a smooth horizontal table. The string passes over a small smooth pulley which is fixed at the edge of the table. Particle B hangs at rest vertically below the pulley with the string taut. Particle A is released from rest. Find the acceleration of Particle B and the tension in the string.

2.3 ANSWERS

Questions 1-6: Check Key Points for answers.

7.

a. Lift problems:

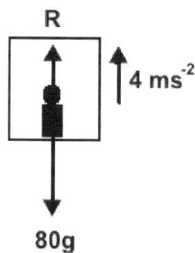

i.   R(↑) R – 80g = ma for the person in the lift moving up

R – (80)(9.8) = (80) (4)

The force of the lift on the person is R = 80 (9.8 + 4)

= 1104 N

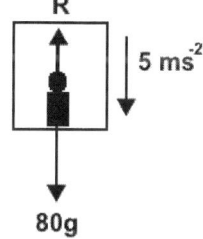

ii. R(↑) 80g - R = ma for the person in the lift moving down

80(9.8) - R = (80) (5)

R = 80 (9.8 – 5) = 384 N

The force of the lift on the person is R = 384N

b. Connected object problems:

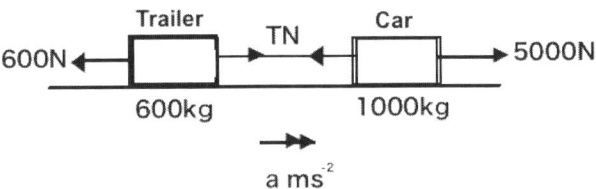

R($\rightarrow$) 5000 – T = 1000a for the car

R($\rightarrow$) T – 600 = 600a for the trailer

Adding the above two equations we eliminate T and get,

5000 – 600 = 1600a

4400 = 1600a

$a = \frac{4400}{1600} = \frac{11}{4} = 2.75 \ ms^{-2}$

Acceleration of the car is 2 .75 m s^{-2}

T – 600 = 600a for the trailer

T = 600(1 + a) = 600 (3.75) = 2250N

The tension in the tow rope is 2250N

c. Problems with a pulley and two objects

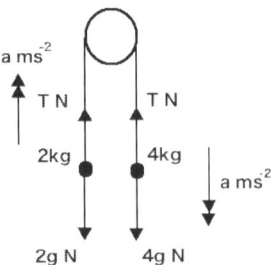

Using $F = ma$ for the 2 kg mass we have

$T - 2g = 2a$

Using $F = ma$ for the heavier 4 kg mass we have

$4g - T = 4a$

Adding the two equations we eliminate T and get

$4g - 2g = 4a + 2a$

$2g = 6a$

$a = 3.27$ ms-2

The acceleration of the system is 3.27 ms-2

 Substituting the value of a in equation $T - 2g = 2a$ we have

$T = 2a + 2g = 26.13N$

The tension in the string is 26.13N.

d. Pulley and table problem

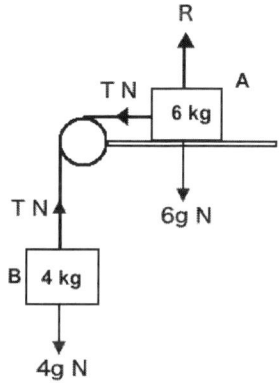

Using $F = ma$ for the particles A and B we have,

For A: $T = 6a$ (no vertical component)

For B: $4g - T = 4a$

Adding the above equations, we eliminate T and get

$4g = 6a + 4a = 10a$

$a = \frac{4g}{10} = 3.92 \text{ ms}^{-2}$

Acceleration of particle B is 3.92 ms^{-2}

Substituting a in equation $T = 6a$ we get

$T = 6(3.92) = 23.52 \text{ N}$

The tension in the string is 23.52 N.

3. FRICTION

3.1 KEY POINTS

1. Types of Forces:

    a. Thrust is the force exerted on an object in order to push the object.

    b. Tension is the force that is transmitted through a string when it is pulled tight by forces acting from opposite ends.

    c. Friction is a force that opposes the motion between two rough surfaces.

    d. Normal Reaction is the support force exerted on an object when it is in contact with another stable object.

    e. Gravity is the force that attracts objects to the centre of the earth. The force of gravity is also the weight of the object.

    f. Air resistance is the frictional force acting on bodies travelling through air.

2. Models and Modelling assumptions.

    a. A particle is a small object of point mass which has no dimensions.

    b. A uniform body is one that has its mass evenly distributed and concentrated at a single point called the centre of gravity.

    c. A light object is an object considered to have zero mass.

    d. A light, inextensible string is one that does not stretch and has zero mass. The tension in the string is constant and masses attached to the ends of the string will move with the same acceleration.

e. A smooth surface is one where there is no friction between the surface and an object moving over it.

f. A rough surface is one where there is friction between the surface and an object moving over it.

g. A thin wire or rod is considered to have zero mass.

h. A smooth and light pulley is considered to have zero mass and presents no friction to a string passing over it. The tension will be the same on both sides of the pulley.

3. Resolution of Forces

a. A single force of magnitude F acting at an angle of θ to the horizontal can be resolved into two components – a vertical component of F sin θ and a horizontal component of F cos θ.

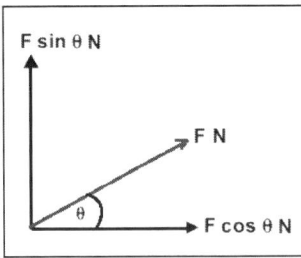

b. The component of the force of magnitude F in a certain direction is F cos θ where θ is the size of the angle between the force and the direction of motion.

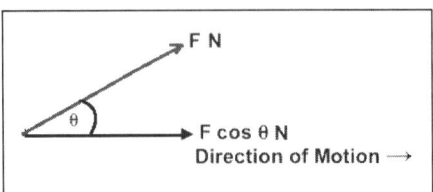

4. Friction

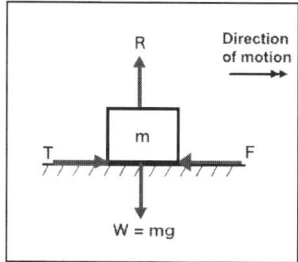

a. The block does not move if $T \le F$ where T is the horizontal force and F is the force of friction.

b. The block moves if $T > F$ where T is the horizontal force and F is the force of friction.

c. When $T = F_{MAX}$, the magnitude of the force T is the maximum or limiting value of the frictional force. The block will remain at rest in limiting equilibrium.

5. The maximum or limiting value of friction between two surfaces in contact depends on:

a. the normal reaction R between the two surfaces

b. the roughness of the two surfaces

6. Roughness is measured by the Coefficient of Friction μ for two surfaces in contact. The rougher the surfaces the larger the μ. Smooth surfaces have $\mu=0$.

7. The maximum or limiting value of the friction F_{MAX} between two surfaces is given by

$$F_{MAX} = \mu R$$

where μ is the coefficient of friction and R is the normal reaction between the two surfaces.

8. Forces at angles: In order to find the magnitude and direction of the resultant of two forces that are at an angle to each other:

a. Construct a parallelogram with the two forces.

b. Draw a diagonal.

c. Use the Cosine rule to find the length of the diagonal – the magnitude of the resultant.

d. Use the Sine rule to find the direction of the resultant.

Example: Two forces P and Q act on a particle. The force P has magnitude 5N and the force Q has magnitude 3N. The angle between the directions P and Q is 40°. The resultant of P and Q is F.

i.   Find the magnitude of F.

ii.   Find the angle between the directions of F and P.

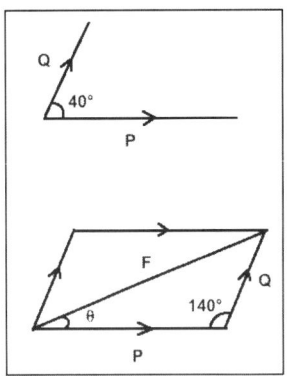

i.   Using the Cosine rule we have,

$F^2 = P^2 + Q^2 - 2PQ \cos 140$

$F^2 = 5^2 + 3^2 - 2(5)(3) \cos 140$

$F^2 = 25 + 9 - 30 \cos 140$

$F = 7.55 \text{ N}$

ii.   Using the Sine rule we have,

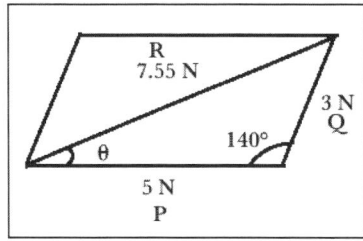

$$\frac{\sin \theta}{3} = \frac{\sin 140}{7.55}$$

$$\therefore \sin\theta = \frac{3 \sin 140}{7.55}$$

$$\therefore \ \theta = 14.8°$$

9. To solve problems about a particle on an inclined plane, resolve the forces parallel and perpendicular to the plane.

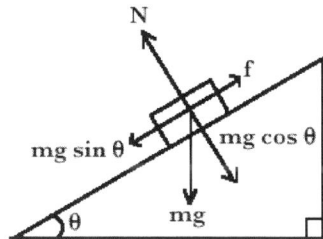

Normal Reaction N = mg cos θ

Frictional force f = mg sin θ

3.2 TEST YOURSELF

1. Define the forces Thrust, Tension, Friction, Normal Reaction, Gravity and Air resistance.

2. Comment on the following modelling assumptions:

    Light, inextensible string

    Smooth, light pulley

    Rough surface

    Uniform body

3. State the two components of resolution of a single force of magnitude F acting at an angle of θ to the horizontal.

4. State the component of a force of magnitude F in the direction of motion where θ is the angle between the force and the direction of motion?

5. For the following system of forces, find the sum of the components in i. the x-direction ii. the y-direction.

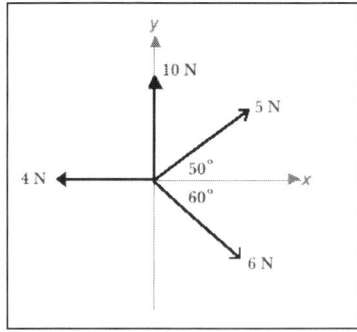

6. If T is a horizontal force pushing an object forward and F is the frictional force between the object and the surface it is on, state the following:

    a. Under what condition is the object at rest?

    b. Under what condition does the object move?

c. State the condition of being at rest in a limiting equilibrium.

7. What 2 factors do the maximum or limiting equilibrium depend on?

8. How is roughness measured?

9. What is the Coefficient of Friction μ for a smooth surface?

10. State the formula for the maximum or limiting value of friction F_{MAX} between two surfaces.

11. State an expression for the normal reaction and the frictional force of a particle of mass m on a plane inclined to the horizontal at an angle of θ°.

12.

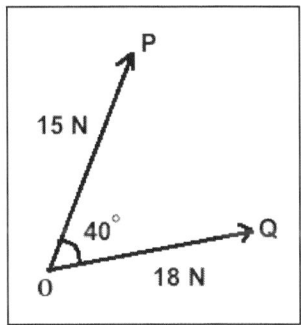

Two forces P and Q act at the point O. Force P has a magnitude of 15 N and force Q has a magnitude of 18 N. The two forces act at an angle of 40°at O.

Find the resultant of the two forces and the angle it makes with the force Q.

13.

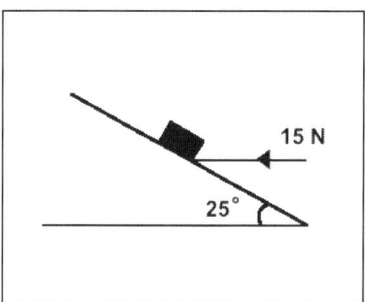

A box weighing 6 kg lies on a rough plane inclined at 25° to the horizontal. The box is held in equilibrium by a horizontal force of magnitude 15N and is on the point of moving down the plane. Find

i.   the magnitude of the normal reaction of the plane on the box,

ii.   the coefficient of friction between the box and the plane.

3.3 ANSWERS

Questions 1-4: Check Key Points for answers.

5.

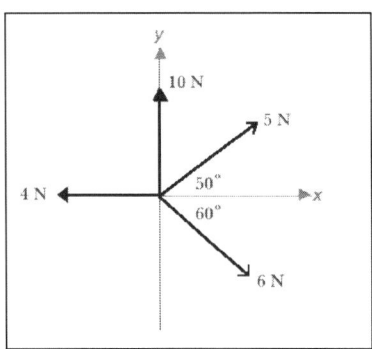

i.   Sum of components of forces in the x-direction are

= 5 cos 50 + 6 cos 60 – 4

= 3.2139 + 3 – 4

= 2.21 N (3 s.f.)

ii. Sum of components of forces in the y-direction are

= 10 + 5 sin 50 – 6 sin 60

= 10 + 3.8302 – 5.1962

= 8.63 N (3 s.f.)

Questions 6-11: Check Key Points for answers.

12.

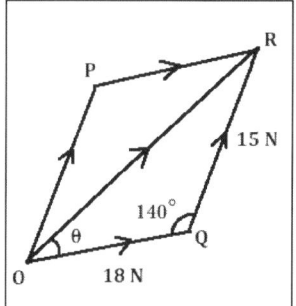

Using the cosine rule we have,

$$OR^2 = 15^2 + 18^2 - 2(15)(18)\cos 140$$

$$OR^2 = 962.66$$

The magnitude of the resultant is given by R

R = 31.0 N

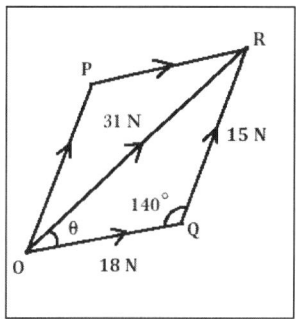

Using the sine rule we have,

$$\frac{\sin\theta}{15} = \frac{\sin 140}{31}$$

$$\therefore \sin\theta = \frac{15\sin 140}{31} \quad \therefore \theta = 18°$$

The angle between the resultant and the force Q is 18°.

13.

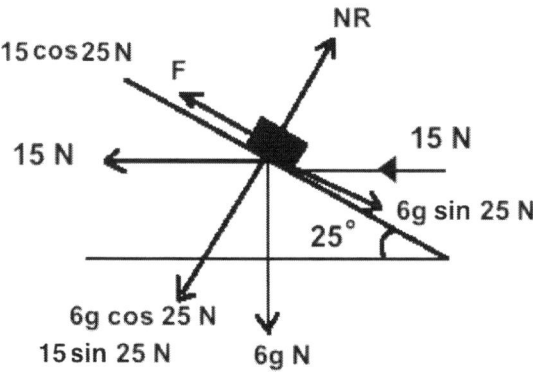

i.   By resolving the forces acting on a particle on an inclined plane we have,

R = 6g cos 25 + 15 sin 25

R = 53.29 + 6.34

R = 59.6 N

Magnitude of the normal reaction of the plane on the box= 59.6N

ii.   We have FMAX = μR

FMAX = 59.6μ

Also FMAX = 6g sin 25 – 15 cos 25

Equating we get,

59.6 μ = 6g sin 25 – 15 cos 25

The coefficient of friction μ = 0.189

4. COLLISIONS

4.1 KEY POINTS

1. The momentum of a particle of mass m kg moving with a velocity of v m s^{-1} is mv N s. The unit of momentum is a Newton second (N s).

2. The impulse of a constant force F acting for a time t is defined as Ft.

3. The Impulse Momentum Principle states that Impulse = Change in momentum

    Impulse = Final momentum – Initial momentum

    I = mv - mu

4. When two bodies collide with each other, the principle of Conservation of Momentum states that

    Total Momentum before impact = Total Momentum after impact

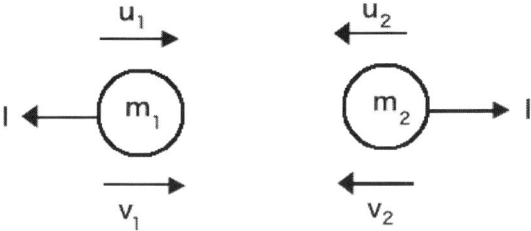

    For two masses m_1 and m_2, with velocities u_1 and u_2 before the collision and velocities v_1 and v_2 after the collision, we have:

    $m_1u_1 + m_2u_2 = m_1v_1 + m_2v_2$

5. When two bodies collide with each other, they exert an impulse on each other of equal magnitude but in opposite directions.

$$m_1v_1 - m_1u_1 = -(m_2v_2 - m_2u_2)$$

6. If two colliding bodies are said to coalesce (merge) after a collision, the principle of Conservation of Momentum becomes:

$$m_1u_1 + m_2u_2 = (m_1 + m_2) v_1$$

4.2 TEST YOURSELF

1. Define the momentum of a particle of mass m and velocity v. What is the unit of momentum?

2. Define the impulse of a constant force F acting for a time t.

3. State the Impulse – Momentum principle.

4. State the principle of Conservation of Momentum of two colliding bodies.

5. Describe the impulse produced by two colliding bodies.

6. State the modified principle of Conservation of Momentum of two colliding bodies that coalesce after collision.

7. Two particles P and Q of mass m kg and 5 kg respectively travel in the same direction on a smooth horizontal plane. P moves with speed 12 ms^{-1} and Q moves with speed 8 ms^{-1}. Immediately after the collision, P is at rest and Q moves with speed 14 ms^{-1}. Calculate the value of m.

8. Two particles of masses 10 kg and 5 kg move on a smooth horizontal plane. They are moving towards each other in the same straight line when they collide. Immediately before the impact the speeds of the particles are 12 ms^{-1} and 8 ms^{-1} respectively. Assuming that the particles coalesce after collision, calculate the speed of the combined particle.

9. Particles P and Q of masses 0.5kg and 0.6kg respectively are free to move in a straight horizontal track. The particle Q is at rest as particle P moves towards Q with a speed of 6 m s^{-1}. After the impact, Q has a speed of 2 ms^{-1}. Find

a. the speed of P after the impact.

b. the magnitude of the impulse of Q on P during the impact.

4.3 ANSWERS

Questions 1-6: Check Key Points for answers.

7.

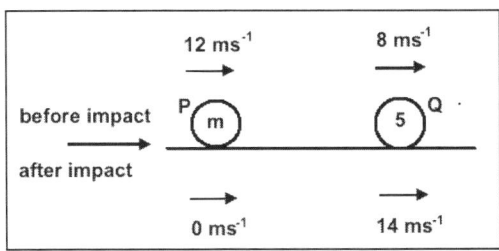

Total momentum before impact $= m_1u_1 + m_2u_2 = (12m + 40)$ Ns

Total momentum after impact $= m_1v_1 + m_2v_2 = 0 + 70$ Ns

$12m + 40 = 70$

$12m = 30$

$m = 2.5$ kg

8.

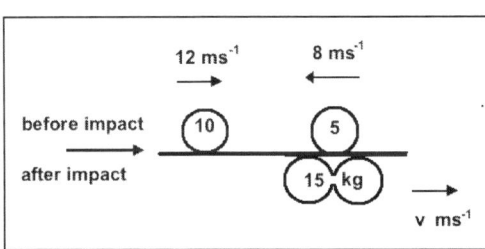

For particles that coalesce we have

$m_1u_1 + m_2u_2 = (m_1 + m_2)$ v

$(12 \times 10) - (8 \times 5) = (10 + 5)$ v

$120 - 40 = 15v$

$$v = \frac{80}{15} = 5.33 \text{ ms}^{-1}$$

9.

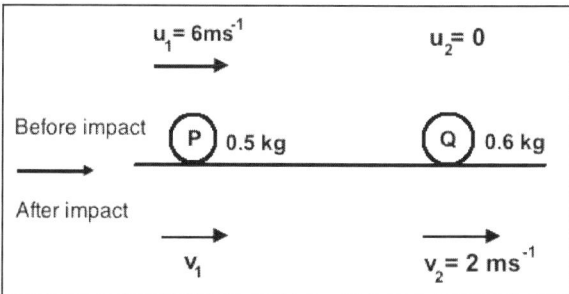

a. Total momentum before impact $= m_1u_1 + m_2u_2 =$
   $6(0.5) + 0(0.6)$ Ns $= 3.0$ Ns

   Total momentum after impact $= m_1v_1 + m_2v_2 =$

   $v_1(0.5) + 2(0.6)$ Ns $= 0.5\ v_1 + 1.2$

   $0.5\ v_1 + 1.2 = 3.0$

   $v_1 = \frac{3.0 - 1.2}{0.5} = 3.6 \text{ ms}^{-1}$

   Speed of particle P after impact $= 3.6 \text{ ms}^{-1}$

b. Impulse $=$ (Final momentum – Initial momentum) for
   particle B

   $I = mv - mu$

   $I = 2\ (0.6) - 0(0.6) = 1.2$ Ns

   The magnitude of the impulse of Q on P during the

   impact $= 1.2$ Ns

5. STATICS OF A PARTICLE

5.1 KEY POINTS

1. For particles in equilibrium:

   a. The resultant of the forces acting on a particle in equilibrium is zero.

   b. The particle in equilibrium remains at rest – there is no motion.

2. To solve problems about particles in equilibrium, follow the steps:

   a. Draw a force diagram or a free body diagram indicating the magnitude and direction of all the forces acting on the particle.

   b. For a particle on a horizontal plane, resolve the forces into horizontal and vertical components.

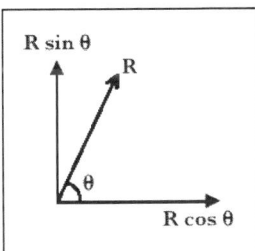

For a particle on an inclined plane, resolve the forces into components parallel and perpendicular to the plane.

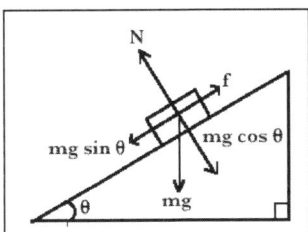

   c. For a particle on a horizontal plane, equate the sum of the horizontal forces and the sum of the vertical forces to zero. For a particle on an inclined plane, equate the sum of the forces parallel to the plane and the sum of the forces perpendicular to the plane to zero.

   d. Solve the two resulting equations to find the unknown forces.

3. When a body is in equilibrium, the frictional force attains a maximum value of μR where μ is the coefficient of friction and R is the normal reaction.

   a. The body is said to be in limiting equilibrium (on the point of moving) if $F_{MAX} = \mu R$.

   b. The body is said to be at rest and in equilibrium if $F_{MAX} < \mu R$

5.2 TEST YOURSELF

1. State two conditions that hold for a particle in equilibrium.

2. List four steps to solve problems about a particle in equilibrium.

3. The diagram shows a particle in equilibrium under the forces shown. Find the magnitude of the force F and the angle θ.

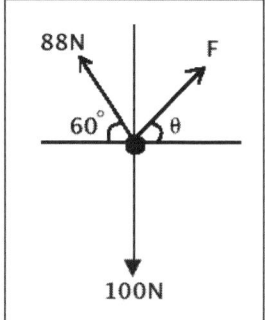

4. The diagram shows a particle in equilibrium under the forces shown. Find the magnitude of the forces P and Q.

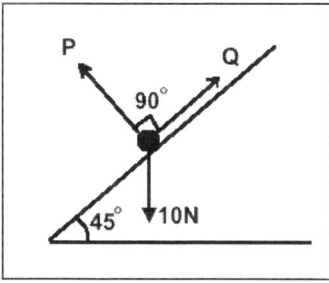

5.

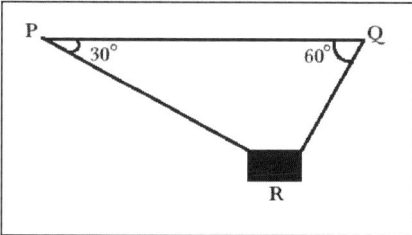

Two ends of a string are attached to two points P and Q of a beam that is fixed horizontally. A mass of 4 kg is attached to the string at the point R. The mass hangs in equilibrium and the string makes the angles 30° and 60° with the beam at P and Q. By modeling the mass as a particle and the string as light and inextensible, find

a. the tension in PR,

b. the tension in QR.

6. Define the frictional force when a body is in limiting equilibrium.

7.

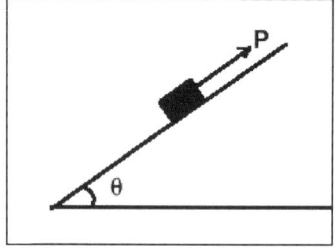

A box of mass 5 kg is placed on a rough plane inclined at an angle θ to the horizontal where $\sin \theta = \frac{3}{5}$. Given that the box is modeled as a particle and that the coefficient of friction is 0.2, find the magnitude of the force P N acting along the plane which is just sufficient to prevent the box from

a. sliding up the plane.

b. sliding down the plane.

8. Two forces A and B act at a point O and are at right angles to each other. A has magnitude of 15 N and B has a magnitude of 8N.

    a. Calculate the magnitude of the resultant of A and B. Calculate the angle between the resultant and the force B.

    b. A third force C is now applied at O. The three forces A, B and C are in equilibrium. State the magnitude of C, and calculate the angle between the forces C and B.

5.3 ANSWERS

1. Check Key Points for answer.

2. Check Key Points for answer.

3.

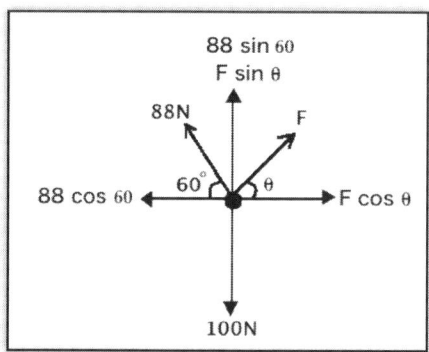

Resolving horizontally we have:

$F \cos \theta - 88 \cos 60 = 0$

$F \cos \theta = 88 \cos 60$

$F \cos \theta = 44$

Resolving vertically we have:

$F \sin \theta + 88 \sin 60 - 100 = 0$

$F \sin \theta = 100 - 88 \sin 60$

$F \sin \theta = 23.7898$

$\therefore \dfrac{F \sin \theta}{F \cos \theta} = \dfrac{23.7898}{44}$

$\tan \theta = 0.5407$

$\theta = 28.399 = 28°$

$F \cos \theta = 44$

$F = \dfrac{44}{\cos \theta} = 50 \text{ N}$

4.

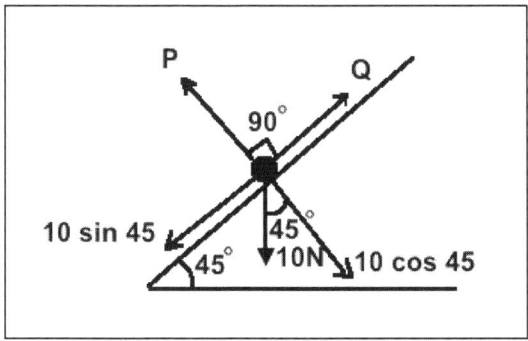

Resolving parallel to the inclined plane we have:

Q – 10 sin 45 = 0

Q = 10 sin 45 = 7.07 N

Resolving perpendicular to the inclined plane we have:

P – 10 cos 45 = 0

P = 10 cos 45 = 7.07 N

5.

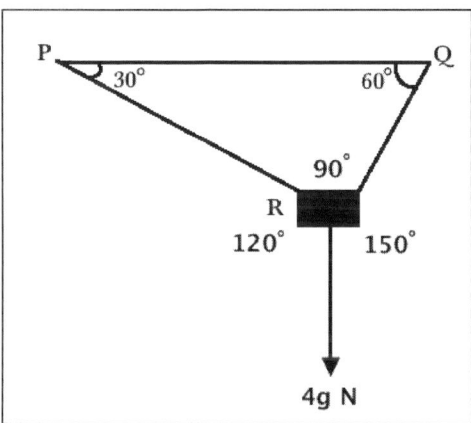

Since the three forces are in equilibrium the following holds:

$$\frac{4g}{\sin 90} = \frac{PR}{\sin 150} = \frac{QR}{\sin 120}$$

a.

$$\frac{4g}{\sin 90} = \frac{PR}{\sin 150}$$

$$PR = \frac{4g\sin 150}{\sin 90}$$

$$PR = \frac{39.2}{2} = 19.6 \text{ N}$$

b.

$$\frac{4g}{\sin 90} = \frac{QR}{\sin 120}$$

$$QR = \frac{4g\sin 120}{\sin 90}$$

$$QR = 39.2 \,(0.8660) = 33.9 \text{ N}$$

6. Check Key Points for answer.

7.

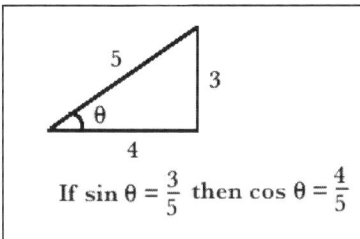

If $\sin \theta = \frac{3}{5}$ then $\cos \theta = \frac{4}{5}$

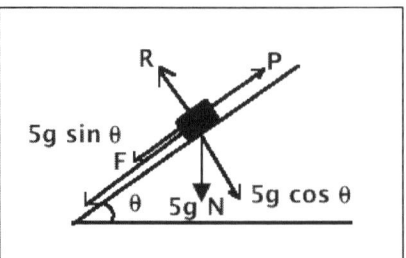

Normal reaction $R = 5g \cos \theta = 5\,(9.8)\,0.8 = 39.2 \text{ N}$

Friction $F_{MAX} = \mu R$

$F_{MAX} = 0.2$ x 39.2 R $= 7.84$ N

a.

   $P - F - 5g \sin \theta = 0$

   $P = F + 5g \,(3/5)$

   $P = 7.84 + 29.4 = 37.24$ N

   $P = 37.24$ N to prevent the particle from sliding up

   the plane.

b.

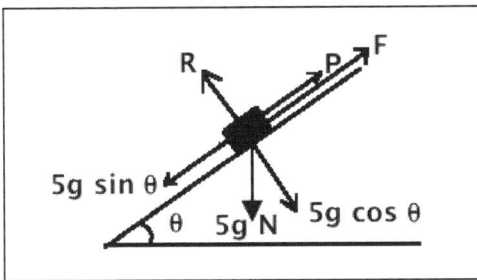

$P + F = 5g \sin \theta$

$P = 5g \sin \theta - F$

$P = 29.4 - 7.84 = 21.56$ N

$P = 21.56$ N to prevent the particle from sliding
down the plane.

8.

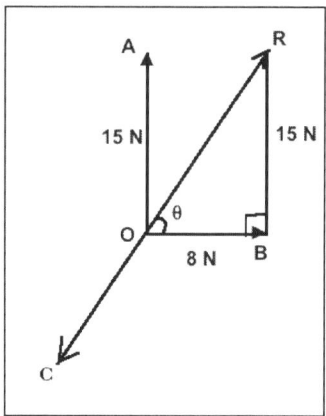

a. Magnitude of the resultant is given by $R^2 = 8^2 + 15^2$

$$R = \sqrt{8^2 + 15^2} = \sqrt{289}$$

Magnitude of the resultant of forces A and B = 17 N

$$\tan \theta = \frac{15}{8} = 1.875$$

$$\theta = \tan^{-1} 1.875 = 62°$$

Angle between the resultant R and the force B is $62°$

b. A, B and C are in equilibrium. Hence it follows that the resultant of A and B is equal to C in magnitude and opposite to C in direction.

The magnitude of force C = 17 N

The angle between the forces C and B = 180 − 62 = $118°$

6. MOMENTS

6.1 KEY POINTS

1. The moment of a force acting on a body is the measure of the turning effect of the force on the body.

2. The units of a moment are Newton-metres (Nm).

3. The moment of a force (Nm) = force (N) × perpendicular distance x from the pivot (m).

    Moment of F about P = Fx Nm clockwise.

    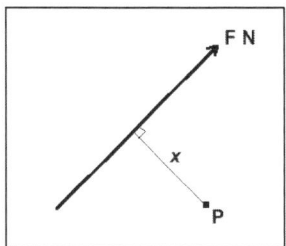

4. Moments can be either clockwise or anticlockwise.

    If the pivot point is to the left of the force, the moment is anticlockwise.

    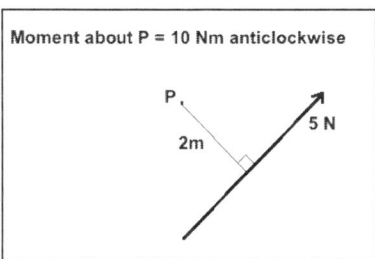

If the pivot point is to the right of the force, the moment is clockwise.

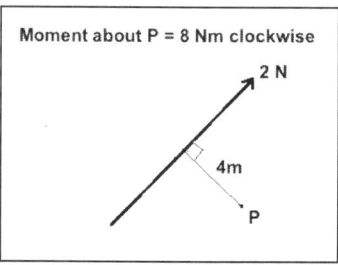

If the pivot point is in the direction of the force, there is no moment.

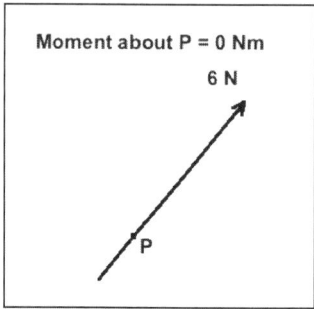

5. When there are several coplanar forces acting on a body, the sum of the moments about a point is given by the difference between the sum of moments in the clockwise direction and the sum of moments in the anticlockwise direction.

Example: The diagram shows a set of forces acting on a light rod. Calculate the sum of the moments about the point P.

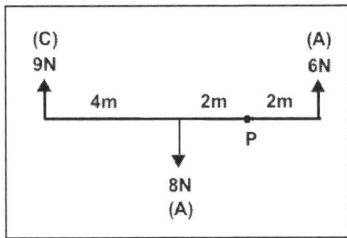

The moment of the 9N force $= 9\,(4 + 2) = 54$ Nm clockwise

The moment of the 6N force $= 6\,(2) = 12$ Nm Anticlockwise

The moment of the 8N force $= 8\,(2) = 16$ Nm Anticlockwise

Sum of clockwise moments $= 54$ Nm

Sum of anticlockwise moments $= (12 + 18) = 28$ Nm

Sum of moments about P $= 54 - 28 = 26$Nm clockwise

6. When a rigid body is in equilibrium under the action of a set of forces, the resultant force in any direction is zero and the sum of the moments about any point is zero. The centre of mass of a uniform rod is at its midpoint.

Example:

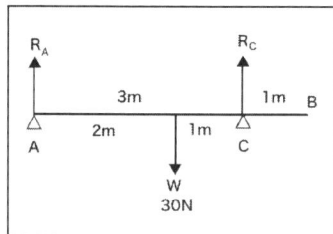

AB is a uniform rod of length 4m and weight 30N resting horizontally on supports at A and C, where AC = 3m. Calculate the magnitude of the reaction at each of the supports A and C.

The uniform rod is at rest or in equilibrium.

Resolving vertically, $R_A + R_C = 30$

Consider the moments about the pivot point A.

For a body in equilibrium, sum of clockwise moments = sum of anticlockwise moments

$(30 \times 2) = R_C (2 + 1)$

$3 R_C = 60$

$R_C = 20N$

We now have $R_A + 20 = 30$

Therefore $R_A = 10N$

The magnitude of the reaction at each of the supports A and C are 10N and 20N respectively.

7. For a non-uniform rigid body, its weight acts at its centre of mass. In the case of a non-uniform rod, the centre of mass is not necessarily at its midpoint but is either specified or will need to be calculated.

Example: A non-uniform rod AB of length 8m is supported horizontally on supports at A and B and the reactions at these supports are 4g N and 6g N respectively. Find the position of the centre of mass with respect to A.

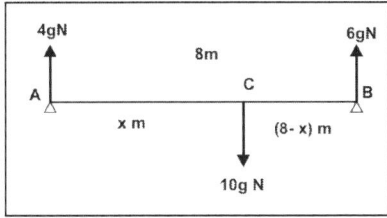

Resolving vertically we have,

Weight $= 4g + 6g = 10g$ N

Let the centre of mass act at a point C, x m from A.

Considering the moments about A and equating the clockwise and anticlockwise moments we have:

$10g\ x = 6g\ (8)$

$x = 48g\ /\ 10g = 4.8$ m

Position C is 4.8 m away from A.

6.2 TEST YOURSELF

1. Define the moment of a force.

2. What are the units of a moment?

3. How is the moment of the force F about the point P calculated?

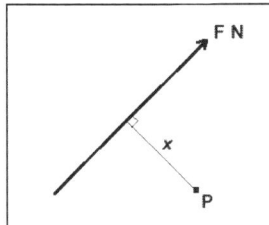

4. State the rotational direction of the moment of a force when the pivot point is a) to the right of the force, b) to the left of the force.

5. When there are several coplanar forces acting on a body, give an expression for the sum of the moments about a point.

6. When a rigid body is in equilibrium under the action of a set of forces, what is the resultant force in any direction?

7. When a rigid body is in equilibrium under the action of a set of forces, what is the sum of the moments about any point?

8. Where is the centre of mass of a uniform rod?

9.

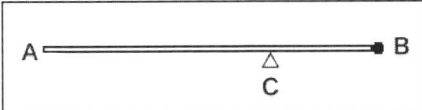

A uniform rod AB has mass 10 kg and length 6 m. A particle of mass 5 kg is attached to the rod at B. The rod is supported at point C and rests in equilibrium in a horizontal position. Find the length of AC.

10. AB is a non-uniform plank of length 6m and weight 150N. The plank is pivoted at its midpoint and is in equilibrium in a horizontal position with a child of weight 100N sitting at A and a child of weight 200N sitting at B. The plank is modeled as a rod and the two children are modeled as particles. Find the distance of the centre of mass of the plank from A.

6.3 ANSWERS

Questions 1-8: Check Key Points for answers.

9.

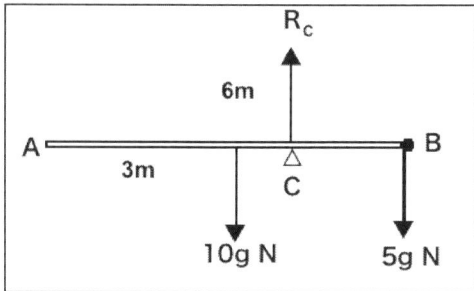

Resolving vertically we have,

$R_C = 10g + 5g = 15g$ N

Taking moments about A

$(10g \times 3) + (5g \times 6) = AC \times 15g$

$30g + 30g = 15g\, AC$

$AC = \frac{60g}{15g} = 4$ m

The length of AC = 4 m.

10.

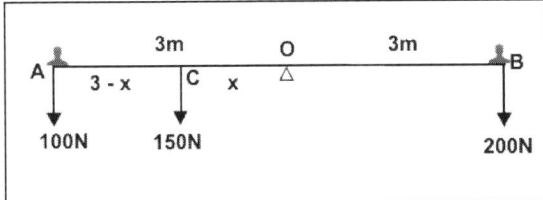

Let x be the distance between the pivot O and the centre of mass C.

Equating the moments about the pivot O, we have,

$150x + 3\,(100) = 3(200)$

$150x = 300$

$x = \dfrac{300}{150} = 2\text{ m}$

Hence the distance of the centre of mass of the plank from A = 3 – 2 = 1m.

ABOUT THE AUTHOR

Shobha Natarajan holds an MSc in Mathematics from Bangalore University and teaches Mathematics to students at A Level and GCSE in the Medway area of Kent. The Maths Clinic was established in 2011 to publish revision guides in Mathematics in print and Kindle e-book format. These books would soon be available as mobile apps on Apple iOS and Android devices. Shobha is a software professional with over 25 years' experience in embedded software development.

www.themathsclinic.co.uk

Printed in Great Britain
by Amazon